Pain With \ In Cornwall

Welcome

Welcome to my poetry
I'm glad that you've dropped in
To share some time together
Just choose where you begin

Most people read from front to back
Some browse the other way
Here you can dip in and out
To suit your mood each day

Glimpses of the times I've lived
Or playfully invented
Are now contained within this book
And joyfully presented

With love,
Eileen

Publisher:
Eileen Crouch
Liskeard, Cornwall PL14 3EP
eileen.crouch@homecall.co.uk

Copyright: © 2015 Eileen Crouch

The author asserts her moral right to be identified as the author of this work

ISBN:978-0-9567062-3-2

A catalogue record for this book is available from the British Library.

Typeset by Carlton Crouch, Liskeard, Cornwall

Printed by: Launceston Print, 38 Pennygillam Way, Launceston, Cornwall

Photos : Front cover - Eileen Crouch
          Back cover - Carlton Crouch

ART SHOW

All Things Bright and Beautiful
the title of the show
interpreting the lyrics
of the hymn that we all know

With photographs and paintings
all beautiful and bright
shelves filled up with craft and jam
made a lovely sight

The show took place at Stuart House
in its exhibition room
the colourful exhibits
dispelling winter's gloom

Talents were inspiring
art classes are now full
they'll fill the art show next New Year
with more that's beautiful

AUTUMN LOVE

Life in a garden starts with a seed
sown to grow in the dark and come to life in spring

Each stage of growth is observed
as individual characteristics emerge

Temperatures rise and maturity brings
colour and flamboyance to dazzle and thrill

It seems that summer will last forever
but all too soon the display begins to fade

As days grow shorter and cooler
Autumn puts on its own exciting extravaganza

The fiery display outshines any other season
crisp air heightens the senses to every nuance of change

In the autumn of our lives
as in the calendar season
spring and summer's treasures are harvested and
in the mellowness of an Indian Summer
an exquisite tapestry is woven to thrill the heart
in an autumn garden of love

BARDS OF THE CORNISH GORSEDH

Bards of the Cornish Gorsedh
Gathering in the county
Honouring those they highly esteem
Who add to our heritage bounty

The echoes of Celtic tradition
Of writing, painting and song
Are acknowledged as being the culture
Cornwall's built its traditions upon

Historians, poets, craftsmen
Architects, performers on stage
All add a fresh contribution
Whatever their background or age

The Gorsedh includes the Eisteddfod
When talents are all on display
Maybe a winner is someone
Who'll become a bard, too, one day

To all of the people in robes of blue
Our thanks for your gifts freely shared
Cornwall is so much the richer
Having people like you who have cared

Talents that rise up in Cornwall
Are spread through our land and worldwide
So come One & All sing the praises of
The Gorsedh and Cornish pride

BENEDICTION

In nature's theatre of sky and sea
its changing performance
is about to present
      eventide's finale

The audience, at one with creation
a tiny speck on the shore
absorbs this
      fleeting moment of time

Sun sets
The stage lights up

Sea reflects
all the shades of the spectrum
emblazoning the sky

elemental colours
   fire
      air
         and water
            drench the soul

Refreshing

Energising

Revitalising

The indigo curtain of night falls,
Stars appear in the moonglow

The colour-refreshed soul rejoices
      The colour-refreshed soul rejoices

BESIDE THE POND

It's peaceful here beside the pond
Observing what is going on
Anticipating something special
That will happen before long

A damselfly is breaking free
From its case of dingy grey
It rests awhile to dry its wings
Then spreads them in display

Its electric blue's incredible
The wings like finest lace
I quickly take some photographs
Before it leaves this place

I don't disturb its habitat
Just simply sit and look
Using my camera to capture it
For my *Magic in Nature* book

BLUEBELL WOOD

April in a bluebell wood
Well-worn path to follow
Off the road and down the hill
A pond lies in the hollow

Up and down the bluebell banks
To get past fallen trees
Camera catching every view
The joyful walker sees

Leaves are bursting on the trees
Pale green against the sky
Sun and shadows play their part
To please the artist's eye

The sound of running water
From the stream now seen below
Adds counterpoint to birdsong
In this lovely springtime show

Welcome to the bluebells
That bloom then disappear
Then faithfully return again
In April of each year

BODMIN MOOR

High on Bodmin Moor - isolated and shrouded in silence
distant views hidden by dark grey clouds
wraithlike through the mist appears an ancient stone circle

drawing the visitor into its mysterious centre
where benign spirits seem to linger

unusually still – not a breath of wind on the evening air
stunted gorse and ground-hugging flowers
suggest a harsher climate

of weather and temperatures that make all living things freeze
raw elements bringing strong men to their knees

but the moor in this quiet mood captivates the soul
could it ever be hostile – inhospitable – treacherous?

its magnetic attraction bids the visitor ...

Return!
not just on quiet days
but when it's wild, wet and windy
- if you dare!

BOUNDARIES

Constituency boundaries are causing quite a fuss
They want to take a chunk of Devon and annexe it to us
Or will it be the other way just as bad for all
If part of us joins Devon and we lose south-east Cornwall

Every county has uniqueness ours is known to all
Why should we surrender it for a hybrid Devonwall?
Let's leave the border where it is where God must have intended
When the Tamar was created and now passionately defended

Folks need to have a sense of place, a place where they belong
A place to fly their county flag and sing their county song
Trelawney's army's slumbering, their motto's *One and All*
They'll rise if they are needed to protect the Duchy of Cornwall

CARNGLAZE CAVERN

Mysterious Cornwall offers many surprises
deep in the countryside the dense woodland rises
a steep lane leads up to a gate that's inviting
the visitors in to see something exciting
A path leads us through to a wonderful cavern
that's now a theatre and a welcoming tavern
the vast auditorium was hand-hewn by men
who were mining the slate – a prized mineral back then

Past dimly-lit tableaux of miners at work
depicting their lives as their ghosts seem to lurk
in the sombre dark shadows down under the ground
where hard work and sorrow were what miners found
We're guided down steps with the aid of a lamp
everywhere's cool and the rock walls are damp
at last on a level we're asked to stand still
then the anticipation turns to a thrill

Lighting is switched on and to our delight
in the grotto we see a lake sparkling and bright
the water is pure and it never runs dry
although it pours into the river nearby
Retracing our steps there's a new treat in store
outside in the woods with their flower-decked floor
we come across fairies – now, can it be true
yes, look! let's find others and play peek-a-boo

They're enchanting to adults and kids' hearts are won
who know they're not real but they really are fun
escaping the real world for make-believe's nice
pretending they're fairies in this paradise
They say it's a fact – there's no reason to doubt
that when the sun sets and the full moon shines out
this woodland will come into life for the night
and fairies will dance 'til the dawn's early light

CHRISTMAS WEATHER 2013

When the autumn weather lasted well into the final month
We were lulled into a false sense that our winter would be mild
Then nature pulled out all the stops with rain and gale-force winds
We were shaken out of lethargy as the weather became wild

Winds whipped up the oceans lashing promenades and cliffs
Teeming rain made walking quite a hazard from the start
Travelling on the roads and rails were rides with unknown ends
Flooded fields and rivers set communities apart

Violent storms uprooted trees and brought the power lines down
Black-outs had to be endured throughout the Christmas break
Friends whose power was not cut off were heroes of the day
Cooking Christmas dinners for us all, then coming in for cake

Non-electric games were played – chess, cards and bagatelle
Lit up by torch and candlelight and warmed by a fire of logs
Our day was really different from the one that had been planned
Gratitude to our hosts and friends, from family and the dogs

CORNISH HERITAGE

Mining demanded great skills to extract
the treasures from under the ground
inventors came up with amazing solutions
to problems the miners had found

Steam driven engines were built large and small
that hauled out the ore and the men
increasing the profitability
of a great thriving industry then

Demands became great in a very short while
for the copper and tin that was mined
cheap labour abroad soon forced our mines to close
and our men found work hard to find

They took their inventions all over the world
and hard rock mines welcomed the men
families soon followed and built their homes there
the Old Country not seen again

They say Cousin Jacks worked down every deep pit
from El Paso to Melbourne Australia
and many skilled people settled in every town
hard work meant no one was a failure

Roots they transplanted have grown a new breed
speaking Cornish with accents quite strange
serving pasties with chillies or kangaroo meat
adapting their customs to change

CORNISH GARDENS

Wonderful Cornish Gardens, I'm glad I live so near
having them on my doorstep I can visit them all through the year
With giant rhododendrons and camellias in the spring
bulbs in great profusion, new life in everything

The magic of a bluebell wood's a challenge to describe
lit up by shafting sunlight, it's the highlight of my ride
Weathered bridges, paths and walls and splendid gatehouse towers
dovecotes, follies, tubs and urns add charm amongst the flowers

High above the Atlantic sea, harsh gale-force winds defying
exotic plants are flourishing that elsewhere may be dying
A garden tumbling down a cliff, steps leading to a bay
another, laid our formally in the fashion of its day

Inspired on foreign travels in Europe and the East
France, Italy, China and Japan add richness to the feast
African and Asian and Southern Hemisphere themes
use giant plants and vibrant flowers to portray the gardeners' dreams

Summer trees and shady walks, a dazzling array of flowers
scent and scene entrance my soul as I while away the hours
It's nice to talk to gardeners who will pass on useful tips
finding out which plants grow best and which have haws and hips

(cont'd)

Herb, vegetable and flowerbeds enclosed within high walls
peaceful lakes, man-made streams and rushing waterfalls
Still warm, as autumn turns the leaves to orange, flame and gold
it's perfect to go picnicking before it gets too cold

The quiet times in winter are more tranquil and I know
it really will be beautiful with a dusting of fresh snow
With every changing season, as the garden scenes unfold
there are wonders to be marvelled at and stories to be told

Of secret gardens, grottoes, wishing wells and even ghosts
We succumb to the enchantment in the company of our hosts
Creators of these gardens couldn't possibly have guessed
how much their work would mean to us we really have been blessed

DAWN

Another new Thursday, an ordinary morn
Then I opened the curtains on a glorious dawn
Earth was still dark – no life yet in sight
Trees silhouetted in dawn's early light

Rainbow-like colours then lit up the sky
A dreamy apparition to my still-sleepy eye
Violet, red, orange merged to yellow and green
Then pale blue and indigo coloured the scene

And just like a jewel in the indigo sky
The diamond-bright Morning Star shone on high
It wouldn't last long so I lingered to gaze
At the sky's living painting designed to amaze

Soon the bright colours dissolve and they change
Into luminous light across all heaven's range
Daylight is dawning and the star's out of sight
Frost has turned everything sparkling and white

At last the sun rises lighting up the new day
Essential to all with its life-giving ray
With heart full of gratitude due thanks are conveyed
To God for the beautiful creation He's made

DECIDUOUS AZALEA
– Cornwall, October 2012

The Azalea's autumn foliage creates a crimson glow
And this year there is something else
That's adding to the show.

Mid-October's frosty nights
Began the change from green
But didn't stop some golden blooms
Insisting to be seen

This year's another miracle
When spring flowers blossomed twice
Although it's very puzzling
It is extremely nice

DEEP IN MY MEMORY

Photographs capture an image
The mind will absorb sight and sound
Ensuring events last forever
In the heart to which they are bound

A choir singing in a cathedral
Made an impression on me
My soul joined the beautiful voices
As they soared like birds flying free

Singing in English and Latin
Enjoyment lit up every face
Performing the beautiful anthems
With innocent charm and grace

Schoolchildren made up the choir
Not one of them over thirteen
The music exploited their talents
As solos were sung in between

The love and the joy felt that evening
Along with the music was sent
Down deep in my memory forever
Creating deep peace and content

"DEHWELANS" – Homecoming

Dehwelans, meaning Homecoming, will happen in the fall
Descendants of the Cornish will be welcomed – *One and All*
Ancestors had a hard life, deep mines they had to work
Boys of eight joined fathers, a fate they didn't shirk

Women were Bal Maidens; young girls learned what to do
Breaking up big lumps of ore – no playtime; pleasures few
When mining slumped in Cornwall their skills went overseas
Rewards gave life a purpose, with masters there to please

No wonder boatloads sailed away to build their lives anew
Folks returning now to see where their forefathers grew
World Heritage Site's its status, reflecting passion and pride,
Mining relics – memorials to men - whose kin have spread worldwide

ELUSIVE WORDS

Trying to find a new way
to write what he must say
To capture the essence of loveliness
the feel of a summer day
The absolute stillness of moonlight
or birds on migration flight
The writer seeks the elusive words
that are jumbled and out of sight

How can he write something new
when everything is old
How can he capture a daydream
in nets that are made of gold
A secret glance between lovers
the delirium of pure joy
Children's sense of wonder
what words will he employ

Sometimes alone and in silence
or out in a noisy crowd
Words come to him from somewhere
or nowhere, but seemingly out loud
The writer's quest is over
from a secret bottomless well
Rise the words that he is seeking
and their magic casts a spell

EMPTY HOUSE

In mourning for previous owners
the house now had no heart or soul
the black empty windows looked blankly
at the garden where time took its toll

The marks where the mirrors and pictures
and shelves that once hung on the wall
are signs of a family's existence
in the living rooms bedrooms and hall

Cupboards are empty and waiting
to enclose lots of somebody's things
an old-fashioned telephone's idle
with no-one to answer its rings

Roof tiles are covered with moss
gutters now leak in the rain
broken gates propped up and useless
that never will be used again

Forlorn and deserted and sad
it waits as the time passes by
for someone who wants to move in
and has enough money to buy

ENCHANTED GARDEN

The garden's a rainbow confection
All colours are sweetly contained
A glorious perfumed enchantment
All here in this secret domain

Through a gate it all changes by magic
Like a fairy tale read long ago
You pass through a cool leafy archway
To the breath-taking scene that's on show

There are statues and fountains and waterfalls
That sparkle like myriad lights
Trees all look very mysterious
And paths lead to all of the sights

A seat in an arbour is waiting
And welcomes the dreamer to stay
Watching the birds and the butterflies
And frogs as they come out to play

It is said that at night when the moon shines
They turn into fairies and elves
The garden becomes a true fairyland
When they have it all to themselves

FASCINATION OF CORNWALL
Water, Rocks and Moors

WATER

Seas around Cornwall for ages have been
The highway for traders, especially for tin
When Joseph brought Jesus it's said to be true
They stayed with the monks on the island off Looe

Seas lap the beaches where families play
In the warm summer sunshine while on holiday
Surfing's more rugged, not for the faint hearted
It can be quite obsessive once you get started

Sailing on lakes provides hours of pleasure
There's plenty to do in pursuit of your leisure
Rivers were channelled to harness their power
For grinding the grain and producing the flour

The Tamar's the border between us and Devon
The bridges bring visitors to our piece of heaven
The Fowey rushes down from its source on the moor
While others flow gently towards the seashore

(cont'd)

FASCINATION OF CORNWALL

ROCKS

There are wonderful rocks on the shore by the sea
Like sculptures in galleries and the entry is free
Grey rocks are striped with red yellow or white
One marvels as each different one comes in sight

Cliffs show how the land moved as time has gone by
Free lessons from nature beneath a blue sky
Buildings of seashore-stone lived in with pride
The quarry is visible with each ebbing tide

These rocks you will only find down on the shore
They change very noticeably up on the moor
Where granite appeals to the stonemason's heart
His skill fashions rock into fine works of art

Miners worked hard bringing ore from below
Ruins commemorate their work long ago
Rocks will keep changing all of the time
But these will endure for your lifetime and mine

(cont'd)

FASCINATION OF CORNWALL

MOORS

For natural Cornwall you needn't go far
Moorland is perfect once you've left the car
Landscapes seem bleak when you first look around
Then you'll be intrigued by what covers the ground

Hawthorn and grasses and gnarled twisted trees
Bending in winds that bring men to their knees
Tors rise from the landscape worn bare by the weather
The scene's sometimes softened by the flowering heather

They're part of our history – the circles of stones
Copper mines quarry sites and derelict homes
Railway tracks rusting now mines have closed down
Made use of by walkers hiking from town

The moorland grows wild and provides perfect cover
For birds, bats and butterflies that they'll soon discover
With wide open skies you can see miles away
And the lure of the moors means you'll come back one day

FEBRUARY FLOWERS

On a February day
That was overcast and grey
What a joy it was to see the flowers appear
Snowdrops' sparkling white and green
For several weeks had been
Braving rain and snow to let us know they're here

Flowers on Camellias now
Give a dazzling bright pink show
They look far too exotic to survive
Tiny Cyclamen I see
'Neath a bare and sleeping tree
And the Crocuses seem glad to be alive

But what surprised me most
Was a package in the post
Bringing lovely Narcissi across the sea
Isles of Scilly scented blooms
Are now shared between my rooms
So their perfume's there wherever I may be

FLIGHTS OF FANCY

When I look at fine art
I imagine I'm part
Of the scene that was
Lovingly painted
And the sound of choirs singing
Can start my dreams winging
As I soar in the spirit
From here on the ground

I get lost in a novel
Maybe live in a hovel
Or travel to places
With strange sounding names
I'm sometimes a fox
Or a lark on the wing
In my daydreams I really
Can be anything

I'm reading space fiction
And tales of the sea
There are plenty of subjects
To interest me
Today's flight of fancy
Takes me to the moon
But I plan to return
By the first day of June

FOGGY DAY IN CORNWALL

Peering through the windscreen
at views we know so well
draped in gossamer fog and mist
enchantment casts its spell

Fiery colours of autumn
hidden from our view
just palest imitations
occasionally breaking through

Memory paints the countryside
as remembered in the past
landscapes bathed in sunlight
summer passed too fast

Mist shuts out outsiders
we share our cosy space
moods defined by music
minds and souls embrace

FULL MOON

Once again it was full moon
the air was clear and bright
there was magic all around us
on that extra special night

We climbed aboard our dreamboat
and sailed up to the stars
leaving Earth behind to visit
Jupiter and Mars

We found that we were playing
upon the Milky Way
joined by guardian angels
who were showing us the way

Castles built of daydreams
floated all around up there
strategically positioned
overlooking starlight square

We visited the cloudbanks
we'd banked our millions there
golden moonbeams love and dreams
enough for all to share

GARDEN VOLUNTEERS

Volunteers in the garden surprise me every year
I haven't planted them myself yet somehow they got here
wild Allium self-seeded in the ancient old stone wall
now it's spreading everywhere wherever bulblets fall

More welcome are the Violets that know no boundary zones
they turn up in the gravel path sweet blooms amongst the stones
Welsh Poppies too broadcast their seeds spreading far and wide
brightening up the garden wherever they reside

Abundant seeds from Primroses sink into the ground
emerging as welcome early flowers when springtime comes around
self-set Aquilegias ensure annual bright displays
of the lovely "grannies bonnets" on warm summer days

Bluebells Foxgloves Campion all grow beneath the trees
Sycamore Oak and Holly start their growth where no one sees
the beauty of ferns and mosses arriving uninvited
plus frogs and insects on the pond can get one quite excited

Nature can manage very well with little effort from us
my natural garden is flourishing and looks quite marvellous
discover with me the alternative to work in advancing years
be content to sit in the sunshine and welcome the volunteers

GARDENING – 2012

2012's a special year
or so the pundits say
I'm noticing what's happening
in my garden day by day

Governed by the sun and moon
the plants will surely show
how cosmic things affect the Earth
which is what I'd like to know

Taking note of how the wise ones
garden by the moon
I'll try to follow what they say
and I'm starting very soon

Progress will be noted
I hope to be amazed
When my harvest exceeds last year
I will shout aloud my praise

GOING HOME

I'm going home, back home to Cornwall
That's the place I yearn to be
I miss the moors and rugged seashore
And long to feel the welcome they'll give me

The winding lanes and Cornish hedges
The wild life, sunshine and the sudden showers
The road-side stalls where I can purchase
Home-grown fruit fresh vegetables and flowers

When I am home, back home in Cornwall
I'll accept the changes made
I'll recognise the way my heart beats
When seagulls cry as daylight starts to fade

The fishing boats and men returning
Their cheerful greeting as they reach the quay
I'll wave to them when I am living
In my own home in full view of the sea

GRANNIES

Long before we start at school
Our Grannies' wisdom starts to fuel
The fire that is already burning
Deep within our souls for learning

Grannies have a treasure chest
Of sayings that bring out the best
In children when they start to squabble
And parents when life starts to wobble

We couldn't always understand
Her somewhat "verbal sleight-of-hand"
But now we've children of our own
We gather the harvest that she's sown

This heritage passed by word of mouth
Is valued widely – north and south
It wont be found in a fine-bound tome
But around the corner in Granny's home

GRIEF

Storm has passed
Peace at last
Damage vast

Felt the sway
Bridge washed away
Fatal Day

Trees are down
Deserted town
Birds have flown

House too wet
To move back yet
Pets at vet

No tears to weep
Grief too deep
Escape in sleep

GUARDIAN ANGEL

Although you may wonder whether it's true
Your guardian angel's there with you
Very near but out of sight
On hand to guide you to what's right

When at the crossroads you may stand
Trust your angel to understand
And help you as you choose the way
To fulfil your life by night and day

No argument or angry voice
To guide you as you make your choice
Even if things may go wrong
You'll cope because you're *angel-strong*

Days of happiness or even strife
Angelic blessings will touch your life
Wherever life's path leads you far and wide
Be glad you've an angel by your side

HARMONY IN THE WORLD

Everyone is a mini-world
in the centre of a universe
where perfect peace can be found
If we really want
to create an ideal world

By being in harmony with all
who orbit around you
and around whom you orbit
your world and your universe
could become heaven on earth

Staying in tune with all creation
enhancing all that is natural
creating beauty to soothe and inspire
spreading love and goodness
will bring harmony

Each of us is unique
and has much to contribute
to bring about a sublime life
making it peaceful, joyful, fulfilling
and harmonious for all

HENRY RICE (1808-1876)
Liskeard's Foremost Architect

Let's take a walk on the Henry Rice Trail
admiring this architect's eye for detail
in Victorian buildings, both humble and grand
built in our town where, enduring, they stand

Lucky for Liskeard that he was around
when mining brought great wealth from under the ground
his inns, homes and chapels, toll houses and banks
are now his memorial, for which we give thanks

As Borough Surveyor he cared for the town
improving conditions as slums came down
his "Nuisance Books" show he reported each case
of conditions where poor had dire hardships to face

The Medical Officer for Health was his friend
and together they worked to establish an end
to sickness and squalor, early death and disease
mains water and sewers the problems would ease

With so many properties to his name
they're all now enshrined in a "book of fame"
describing the style, size and purpose of each
extolling his standards – still worthy to teach

From the centre of town – north, south, east or west
you will see Henry's buildings stand out from the rest
our respects can be paid for the service he gave
in the graveyard at Lanchard where lies his grave

HEY DAD !

Hey, Dad!   I've found some pennies – are they rare?
Hey, Dad!   Will I become be a millionaire?
Hey, Dad!   I scored the winning goal today
Hey, Dad!   Are you coming out to play?

Life's exciting and so full of fun –
Each day's an adventure for my young son, he says,

Hey, Dad!   Let's search for treasure on the sand
Hey, Dad!   I want to join the silver band
Hey, Dad!   Will we be going to the moon?
Hey, Dad!   Isn't Christmas coming soon?"

Dirt and cuts on his knees and his chin
He runs up to me with a cheeky grin and says,

Hey, Dad!   Mum screamed when my pet mouse got free
Hey, Dad!   What's at the bottom of the sea?
Hey, Dad!   I really don't like school at all
Hey, Dad!   I hope I'll soon be six feet tall"

That's what life's like with my small boy,
A jumble of daydreams and fun and joy.

HIDDEN GARDEN, Stuart House

Contained within formal box hedges
Are perennial flowers and bay trees
Depicting a gentleman's garden
Where everything's planted to please

The seventeenth century-style garden
Welcomes the visitors in
To enjoy all the seasonal flowers
And the fountains to be found within

Leaving behind sounds of traffic
It is blessedly quiet and serene
Here you'll be served with refreshments
With luck there'll be scones jam and cream

Annual displays by the Sealed Knot
The brave costumed women and men
Recalling that King Charles lodged here
When battles were fought way back then

The door to the garden is open
Free to all who can make time to stay
Where enjoyment of seasonal changes
Create daydreams that change every day

HOLDING HANDS

The first time that you clutched my hand
We were crossing a busy street
You laughed when breathlessly I said
I'd been literally swept off my feet

Having safely avoided the traffic
You loosened your vice-like grip
Now that the ice had been broken
We held hands for the rest of the trip

We love holding hand when we're out
Or when watching a film indoors
It always feels so nice and special
Just warming my hand in yours

When sad, just a soft gentle squeeze
Will send out a sign that you're caring
In joy hands pass unspoken feelings
Of pleasures that we are both sharing

We recognise each others sorrows
And the need for a hug and a kiss
Our hands send a very clear message
Of worry elation or bliss

Forever our love and our lives
Will be safe in each others hands
Our commitment was sealed long ago
By exchanging two gold wedding bands

HOLIDAY IN CANADA

Visiting Canada
Vancouver's crystal towers, racoons and summer flowers
Chinatown, English Bay, the Steam Clock chiming hours
how lovely they were

Watching the harbour lights
Grouse mountain's July snow, the loggers' brilliant show
the Bridge at Capilano and the river way below
the tree walk was fun

A day at Fort Langley too
its place in history is there for all to see
at Bear Creek we rode horses on a trail far from the sea
just like pioneers

Wonderful Harrison
the hot springs swimming pool - sand sculptures there were cool
at Hope the chainsaw carvings were all so beautiful
impressed? yes, we were!

Returning to Chilliwack
where I lived long ago while England fought its foe
the memories come flooding back that never let me go
I'm back there again

Reunions in Canada
at Campbell River, too, where family and crew
got to know each other and we raised a glass or two
I'll never forget

HOLIDAY MAGIC

The airport at night
They're calling our flight
And we will soon fly away
Away from the bay
Where we've been to stay
On holiday

Mornings were fine
Golden sunshine
Lazing the hours away
Afternoons, too,
Spent there with you
On holiday

Dancing and dining
Moonlight and wine
Holiday magic
Enchanted this heart of mine

When summer's gone
Memories live on
And we'll recall every day
'Til once again
We're off in a plane
On holiday

ON HOLIDAY

HYACINTHS

I was given some hyacinths in a pot
By someone who knew they'd be loved a lot

Placed in my kitchen I'd watch every day
Amazed at the growth that was soon underway

At first, an inch tall and still tightly curled
The changes were rapid as leaves were unfurled

In a very short while the green buds turned pink
I watched with delight as I worked at the sink

Then as the flowers started to bloom
Their beautiful fragrance spread through the room

Each New Year I welcome the hyacinth's scent
And the promise of spring after winter is spent

I'LL NEVER FORGET CANADA

A town in the Fraser Valley in the province of B.C.
Was where we were sent in wartime - two of my brothers and me

Our family stayed in West London where air raids and fear were endured
For the duration we settled in the haven our journey secured

The blackout became a dim memory - lights could blaze in our new town
As guests we were made very welcome by the family who made us their own

After the war we returned to a bomb-scarred and sad looking land
What a change from the beautiful valley the mountains and forests so grand

Just like a favourite movie, in daydreams my mind often strays
To the scenes of my childhood adventure in those long-ago golden days

IN MY GARDEN – JANUARY 2012

In New Year when the gardens
are most usually sleeping
a close inspection can reveal
some early flowers peeping

As well as winter Heathers
Snowdrops raise their dainty heads
and one dwarf Rhododendron
is fully out ... it's red

Dainty little Cranesbills
can't wait 'til May to bloom
and Camellia "Donation"
offers blossoms for my room

Mahonia's yellow flowers
are attracting birds to feed
there are mauve flowers of the Hebe
and a Dandelion weed

A solitary Primula
and a Crocus now appear
they will soon be joined by others
as we progress through the year

I.T. WIZARD

My clever teenage grandson
Is a wizard at I.T.
When I have a problem
He comes and rescues me

The cursor moves like lightning
As he sorts out my mistakes
His fees are very reasonable
A drink and some chocolate cakes

I know I'll never be a whiz
But still I persevere
Just tailoring my output
To some simple software gear

Perhaps he'll be the next Bill Gates
And take the world by storm
Familiar with technicalities
That to him will be the norm

In the meantime he is dealing
With each problem that arises
Honing skills that may lead the way
To some of life's glittering prizes

IT'S SUMMER

All in the garden is still
Wet leaves glisten in the morning sun
The only movement – a raindrop
falling from a flower

The storm has passed
The garden is resting
after being tossed around
for days by relentless wind
and rain that poured
then poured again

Sky now bright blue
Air wonderfully fresh
Road and paths washed clean
Earth soaked
Plants nourished

It's summer

JANUARY CAMELLIAS

My friend gave me a posy
Of Camellias – vibrant pink
They were growing in her garden
Such a lovely gift, I think

The weather has been wintry
Dawn revealed the frost and ice
Yet early in the new year
These Camellias look so nice

Treasures that were locked up safe
In Mother Nature's banks
Are now released and freely shared
For which our grateful thanks

KNOWING

If lonely and alone through life you walk
And no-one's by your side with whom to talk
Link up to One who wears the mystic crown
Who can cheer you if you're ever feeling down

You needn't wait to go to church on Sunday
You can share your pain and troubles any day
Pour out your heart and face your deepest fears
Feel them dissolve as you shed healing tears

We are born with what can only be called *Knowing*
That an unseen power keeps the life force flowing
With the sun the moon and nature all around
We can marvel at the wonders to be found

Though it's easy to shut out the voice of reason
Especially in a celebratory season
Calm your body and your mind and wear a smile
Remembering what you *Know* for just a while

Take some time out every day for meditation
Close your eyes and lose yourself in contemplation
Open up your heart and soul and you will find
Many blessings of the most enriching kind

LISKEARD OLD CORNWALL SOCIETY
85th Anniversary

Eighty-five years of our O.C.S.
Proclaims it has been a resounding success

Our "Fragments" are archived in Liskeard these days
At Stuart House where they delight and amaze

In documents, photos, recordings and more -
A treasuretrove's waiting for you to explore

History of mining is valued today
As well as the arts – expressed every way

Ancient stone monuments were bought in the past
Ensuring that they would be safe and would last

Memories of members are other archives
Of "Fragments" they've gathered all of their lives

Sharing their pride in this kingdom of old
There are "Old Cornwall" stories yet to be told

No need to be "Old" or be born in this land
To find that to live here is perfectly grand

There's more to discover, so come One and All
And enjoy all the history of Old Cornwall

LIVING THE DREAM

Where did my sense of freedom go?
Elusive at present, but this I know –
Though a captive of duty and daily routine
Some day I'll pursue my ultimate dream

To wander and wonder in places abroad
Seeking out beauty will bring its reward
To experience music I've not heard before
And great works of art to be seen by the score

Free of my bondage, taking delight
Sharing my joy wherever I might
With the one that I love anywhere in the world
As our life of discovery's slowly unfurled

'Til then we've spent time at Port Isaac Bay
The Tate at St.Ives and walking Saints Way
Tintagel, Cotehele and Mt.Edgcumbe are some
Of the places we visited not far from home

Sunny or rainy we really don't mind
Whatever the weather there's so much to find –
Fulfilling the dream and making it true
Right here in Cornwall – just me with you

LOVE AND BEAUTY

Love and beauty have now become the focus of my life
No longer watching T.V. news that's full of war and strife
I wander in my garden aware of what is growing
Or spend some time beside the stream where pure clear water's flowing

If painting flowers does not achieve a masterpiece for me
I'll use a camera to record the perfect blooms I see
I'll choose sweet words to write an ode of love to sweethearts all
And observe the seasons come and go from wintertime to fall

You're welcome to share my dreamboat drifting through the days
Looking through rose-tinted glasses or an early morning haze
It may not change the world for all but still it's right for me
To appreciate love and beauty wherever I may be

MAGIC OF A ROSE BUSH

When I looked at the dead-looking plant for sale
With description doing its best to regale
Only prior experience could make me suppose
It would really become a magnificent rose

I planted and watched it grow week by week
My care and attention was all it would seek
By summer its leaves sprouted healthy and green
In which lots of flower buds could be seen

Vigorously growing, its succession of blooms
Offered beautiful flowers to display in my rooms
There were even enough to give to my friends
Joy from this rose bush it seems never ends

The rose is called Birthday Girl and if you're inclined
To buy one for yourself it is hoped you will find
Rewards far exceeding what I can convey
In this poem of praise written for my birthday

I'm so pleased that a few fading flowers remain
Defying the gale-force winds and the rain
It's surprising to me and to those who remember
As my birthday is not 'til the month of November

MAKEOVER

Our old house was built long ago
Home to various families for years
It now looked its age and was shabby
And a survey confirmed all our fears

From top to the bottom it needed repairs
There were new regulations to meet
Once all of the jobs had been listed
We knew it would be quite a feat

Watching the popular TV shows
Where schemes and ideas abound
We spent time in planning and drawing
Then invited professionals around

The moss was removed from the roof tiles
The gutters lost their dirt and grime
Walls were washed down and then painted
Soon reflecting men's effort and time

Driveway and paths became weed-free
Trees pruned and the garden made neat
It's a home we can be very proud of
Now the makeover's complete

MAN AND HIS BOAT

The river rushes down to the sea
Easy rowing on the ebb tide
Returning on the flood
Leisurely, peacefully
Softly dipping oars
He's in his element
Alone

Observing his world of
Changing seasons
Changing flora and fauna
Changing
Self

Life renewing
On the river
Along the shore
Within
Himself

Alone – not lonely
At one with his world
Ever seeking and finding
Contentment

MARY NEWMAN'S GARDEN

Wonderful Cornish Gardens
not every one is vast
Mary Newman's garden in Saltash
conjures romance and tales of the past

Back in the fifteen hundreds
this was her childhood home
then, as wife of a sea-faring husband
she spent many hours here alone

He sailed with her father, a captain
who admired her young man, Francis Drake
from here in the garden she'd watch as they sailed
from the Tamar – their fortunes to make

Now restored, as it's thought Mary knew it
the garden's secrets unfold
passing perfumed herbs we climb the steps
to a lawn with a view to behold.

A shady arbour, a garden seat
bid the visitor *look at the view*
the glorious Tamar, the people, the ships
and the new things – not one bridge, but two

Mary's vigil can just be imagined
watching for sails to appear
which announced the return to the harbour
of the two men whose lives she held dear

It's a garden for dreaming of past times
while the same sun still shines above
and the Tamar flows out to the sea, as it did
when the Drakes were young and in love

MINING LANDSCAPE

Ruins of copper mines on Caradon Hill
Evocative subjects for artists who will
Paint pictures that capture not only today
But the spirit of past times now faded away

Photographers too love the harsh ruined stacks
Contrasting with moorland and old railway tracks
Skies bright and sunny or darkened with rain
Whatever the weather you'll come back again

Preserving the landscape for all who come here
To the top of the world where the air's fresh and clear
"World Heritage Site" says it's not been in vain
A welcome awaits those who visit again

MOYCLARE

Moyclare's a beautiful garden
Not grand like the National Trust
But a house past the station at Liskeard
Where a regular visit's a must

Created by both of the owners
From a bare building site long ago
Now trees tower over the rooftop
Huge shrubs fill the spaces below

At present a new generation
Look after the garden with care
Opening it up to the public
Whose love of the place they all share

It reaches its peak in the springtime
When shrubs are all fully in bloom
And plants are for sale with the tea and the cakes
In the visitors' garden tea room

MUSIC OF LOVE

Love is ... Lovely
Holding hands
Kissing lips
Embracing arms
Sweet words
a serenade

Love is ... Exciting
Beating hearts
Pulses racing
Thrilling feelings
Magic moments
a rhapsody

Love is ... Ecstacy
Wild emotions
Burning passion
Crescendo
Tempos changing
the finale

MUSICIAN, The

Although you said you loved her
You said you couldn't stay
You had a load of things to do
And songs you had to play

You hadn't time to keep in touch
But she knew where you were
Your band found fame and fortune
You were constantly on tour

You've realised your wildest dreams
You seem to have it all
But your melancholy love songs say
Life isn't all a ball

MYSTERIES

Just imagine how people who lived long ago
Studied stars and created their likeness below
Monoliths altars and circles of stone
Acknowledging that our planet Earth's not alone

Charting the heavens to traverse their way
Recording the sun and the moon rise each day
People would gather on each Solstice morn
Rejoicing to see the sun rise with the dawn

They worked out astronomy and just for good measure
Named all the stars we now study at leisure
Animal shapes reproduced on the ground
Which modern truth seekers remarkably found

The Great Bear the Little Bear the Lion and Hare
Outlined on Cornwall's map show they are there
Disguised in the land its secrets of old
Have now been discovered and in books retold

MY ACERS

They may not be ancient like oak trees or ash
But the Acers in Cornwall get my *winners sash*
They're great in the gardens giving seasonal displays
Providing much pleasure in so many ways

Each Spring Brilliantissima's pink buds burst forth
Proclaiming their brilliance for all they are worth
Dissectum is purple and doesn't grown tall
Its leaves turn to bright red and curl when they fall

Crimson King's handsome 'til leaves tumble down
And lie dry and crunchy, fading to brown
Later in autumn as the weather gets cold
October Glory turns to pink red and gold

Eventually the "glory" tree becomes brilliant red
Blanketing the ground with its colourful spread
The final performance of dazzling displays
Is by Ozakazuki in November's short days

Our Ozakazuki was hard-pruned last year
Had we been over-zealous was our one great fear
It was late growing twigs on which new leaves could sprout
Our worries proved groundless when at last they came out

(cont'd)

Although twigs and leaves were quite slow to appear
By summer their growth had moved into top gear
Clothing the tree in glorious light green
One of the prettiest sights it's been

Then later this year we had downpours non-stop
Most leaves became sodden before they could drop
When gales came they finished them off in one blow
To lie in wet heaps on the ground below

As winds blew and shook other trees until bare
Leaves on Ozakazuki stayed green and hung there
Until mid-December when frost came one night
To turn leaves to gold – a magnificent sight

Just ten days to Christmas it didn't seem right
For leaves on an Acer to create such a sight
Long may they last cheering winter's grey days
They deserve admiration and poems of praise

MY ACERS – Adieu "October Glory"

I planted my Acers a long time ago
And have marvelled each year at their beautiful show
Late in the autumn as days became cold
October Glory turned to pink red and gold

I was sad when the October Glory came down
After many years gloriously wearing its crown
I'd planted it near the house where I could see
But had not envisaged how big it would be

It was too near the house, and too near the drive
Too big to transplant – it wouldn't survive
Cut down, it was valued by a woodworking friend
Though gone from the garden, it wasn't the end

Seasoned and turned into beautiful art
It now gives much pleasure as it plays a new part
Plus, shoots are now sprouting from out of the ground
Once more I'll find "Glory" leaves all around

NEW BEGINNINGS

In the family's photo album I can see
Every new beginning that affected me
The baby quite content on mother's knee
My first appearance on the family tree

The schoolgirl wearing uniform – now older
Having learnt a thing or two is looking bolder
Her schoolwork tucked into a cardboard folder
She is taller, almost up to mother's shoulder

Very shortly after graduation day
A high tech job meant there would be good pay
My motto was *Aim high at work and play*
Embracing life and all that came my way

Pictures catch our joyful wedding from the start
The day I said *I do* to my sweetheart
Truly caught by Cupid's perfectly aimed dart
Meant our happiness could never fall apart

As the years went by and I became a mother
First a daughter then quite soon her little brother
They are gone, we're left alone with one and other
Retired and now called Grandpa and Grandmother

NEW HOME

The house that had been cold and empty
is warm and now once more alive
it loves its new family that lives indoors
and the friends who arrive in the drive

Ceilings and walls freshly painted
the mirrors and pictures and books
are all now in place as are carpets and rugs
coats and hats hanging up on their hooks

Cupboards are no longer empty
they hold lots of everyone's things
and the new telephone's standing ready
for someone to answer its rings

The greenhouse will yield lots of goodies
fresh veggies the aim - every day
flowers will grow in abundance
now the dog has his own space to play

With each alteration completed
the house and the garden looked better
becoming the dream home they wanted
their plans carried out to the letter

NOVEMBER IN THE GARDEN 2011

Gardening in November was unusual this year
Everytime I moved dead leaves spring flowers would appear
Primroses' pretty flowers brought the promise of next spring
That wasn't all – there were more plants that were *keen to do their thing*

Bergenia, with its elephant ears, was blooming once again
And Begonias, pink and red and white, defied the wind and rain
Hydrangeas and Hypericum were just as bright as ever
And Roses kept on flowering, too, regardless of the weather

Siberian Irises thought that they'd put on a second show
The Fuchsias' red and purple flowers maintained their youthful glow
Cranesbills, Cistus, Primula and Campion now flower
Loganberries and Strawberries bloom but their new fruits are sour

Nasturtiums keep on blooming and so does Morning Glory
The lawns are fresh and green – cutting them's another story
Helianthemum, June-flowering, are once again displaying
As are Crinodendron's blooms – what game is Nature playing?

Although they are all lovely, there is one thing that I fear
If we're having spring in Autumn – what will we have next year?

NOW I AM OLD

Now I am old, wear out-of-date clothes
With hats that defy fashions trends
I spend all my pension enjoying myself
Eating and drinking with friends

I only do gardening when inspired
And when warmed by the rays of the sun
I delight in the birds and the butterflies
And put up my feet when I'm done

Each day that I garden and potter
I dream of the harvest to come
And the shows with my produce on display
With prizes awarded for some

Being a heritage item myself
I am here in my private collection
My memory is long - I could tell you a tale
If you'll listen to my recollection

OLYMPIC TORCH RELAY Day 1, 19th May 2012

On the day the Olympic Torch came through
Not only was Town dressed in red white and blue
But Cornwall's sports colours of black and gold
Flew overhead pleasing young and old

Liskeard's Mayor opened events for the day
The Silver Band got the Parade underway
All through the day music played sweet and loud
A great party atmosphere enlivened the crowd

Stuart House Art Centre opened all day
Where refreshments were served so the people could stay
To visit the house with its Craft Sale downstairs
Art in the Gallery and Heritage upstairs

Our musician played all day long out in the sun
Entertaining the visitors who were all having fun
They danced they took photos of the famous Sealed Knot
Did Cornwall set a record for cream teas, or not?

Performances in the park and on the stage too
At museum and school there was plenty to do
Until the Torch Relay Team's time drew near
Then everyone lined the route ready to cheer

At last our reward as the escorts appeared
Policemen on motorbikes and sponsors were cheered
Support cars and buses then the Torch Bearer came
To a rapturous welcome as we witnessed the flame

Thousands in Cornwall enjoyed that first day
Of the 8000 mile journey of the Torch Relay
The Torch cast a spell on the crowds gathered there
As it spread joy and happiness to all everywhere

ON A SUNNY DAY

I used to lie in sunshine getting tanned
Today the threat of cancer says that's banned
So where I now recline is cool and shady
Respectably covered, like a lady

From here I gaze upon the sunlit scene
Time stands still while I eat strawberries and cream
Meditating on past sunny afternoons
Memories flood back like favourite tunes

I am young and we are playing on the beach
The detail's blurred and slightly out of reach
There is laughter, there is fun and there is joy
I feel the love we knew as girl and boy

Days we cycled in the sun to be together
Blazing sun or rain, we just ignored the weather
Pictures flash before me on a bright sunbeam
Fragmented like reflections in a stream

A sudden breeze disturbs my reverie
I reluctantly come back where there is just me
But you're never far away 'cause it would seem
We can meet again if only in a dream

ON THE OCEAN OF LIFE

When we are born
We are cast adrift on the ocean of life
Our training ship may prepare us for the journey
More likely there will be no instruction course
Experience will be our teacher
As captain or crew or maybe both

Single-handed can be perfect
Depending on vessel and goals
A reliable crew is essential
When tackling the world
The ocean of life's never still
With tides ever ebbing or flowing
Squalls erupt suddenly
Storms brew and wreak havoc

The lull afterwards reveals the flotsam and jetsam
Cruising calm waters is balm to the travel-weary
Restoring body and soul
Then, once again,
Searching for the thrills of life
The challenge is resumed
Confronting the elements – surviving

While strength and resources last
The quest continues
Until age decrees a tranquil sea, quiet havens
And shelter from the tempest
A time for memories of the journey
That colour the yarns of the landlubber

ONLY A FRAGMENT

Mid September afternoon
A footpath through the trees
Past Daphne DuMaurier's former home
Just a short walk to the sea

To a fragment of Cornwall's coastal path
High above the sea below
Seascapes sparkling in the sun
Sailing boats graceful and slow

Some wonders of Cornwall are hidden
That a first glance leaves concealed
But with time to explore bays and byways
All its wonders are revealed

By joining up all of the fragments
It's amazing just what will appear
A glorious montage emerges
As changes take place through the year

PARIS IN SPRING

We went to Paris by Eurostar
The weather was warm and sublime
Perfect for all of the tourists
On holiday at Easter time

A boat took us under the bridges
On a trip down the famed River Seine
We took pictures of all of the details
To take home and look at again

At the same time with school friends in Paris
Our granddaughter stayed with the choir
Performing in Chartres old Cathedral
Songs written to thrill and inspire

We heard their performance in Paris
Then at Disney they finished with fun
Their musical gifts freely given
Had blessed and impressed everyone

Our final night out at a nightclub
With its dazzling and elegant show
Added contrasting musical memories
Of the Paris we'd now got to know

PERFECT DAY IN CORNWALL

A sublime September Sunday
blue skies up above
non-stop drive to Mounts Bay
a place we really love
Marazion's our first stop
St Michael's Mount in view
Lord St Levan's home on top
cut off by the tide 'til two

Ferries buck the choppy sea
so ashore we have to stay
we'll have to come another time
to walk the dry causeway
Penzance bids us linger
for a drink and a fine Sunday roast
with unbroken views from the window
of all of this wonderful coast

Newlyn's not far for a walk
the fishing fleet lies in the bay
boats are all so photogenic
we could stay for the rest of the day
but around the bay Mousehole's waiting
harbour walls guarding this nook
superior cats are lying around
one looks like the cat in the book

Mid-afternoon sun is cooling
it's time that we called it a day
Cornish cream teas will be perfect
before we set off on our way
as we travel the final few miles
and twilight bids daytime goodnight
a perfect day's coming to an end
now that our home's in sight

PERFECT VISION (Him)

When I hear your voice shivers run down my spine
Your face and your features are simply divine
You can't know how much seeing you means to me
Your manners are charming, you're delightful to see
Your eyes are hypnotic whenever you smile
In a *handsome men's* contest you'd win by a mile
I couldn't ask more because you are supreme
You are perfect beyond my impossible dream
Whatever smart gear you have chosen to wear
Is perfect for you – my opinion I'd share
But I cannot tell you 'cause we've never met
For I only see you on my television set

PERFECT VISION (Her)

When I hear your voice shivers run down my spine
Your face and your figure are simply divine
I know no other whom I can compare
With your charming manner and beauty so rare
Your beautiful eyes shine whenever you smile
In a contest of beauty you'd win by a mile
I couldn't ask more because you are supreme
You are perfect beyond my impossible dream
Whatever you wear is my favourite dress
You are a vision a lovely goddess
But I cannot tell you 'cause we've never met
For I only see you on my television set

PORTAS PILOT SCHEME
A poetic review – September 2013

Mary Portas believes in the High Street
and she offered her ideas for change
That could revitalise the retail shops
with solutions of wide-reaching range
Liskeard is one of the Pilot towns
to participate in this scheme
Awarded a hundred thousand pounds
could it really fulfil every dream?

Town Team met Mary and showed her around
there was much to be done, she could see
As a start she invited the volunteers in
to start painting the shops – for free
Benches for visitors and flowers appeared
shop windows were filled up with stock
Musicians and dancers performed in the street
giving shoppers a bit of a shock

There was no magic wand – just work and goodwill
and a wish for the plan to succeed
The Town Team now sits on the Council
a position from which they can lead
Mary's programme highlighted a few shops when
in Spring, it was shown on T.V.
Now visitors to the town say they have come
to find out what else they can see

(cont'd)

With a Charter that dates back hundreds of years
a market's been held here non-stop
Then mining for copper on Caradon Hill
gave Victorians money to shop
Nestled in Cornwall, surrounded by sea,
farms, moors and the big open skies
Once more we will make it a town of renown
to discover by all, with surprise

Food, flowers, books, clothes and T.V.s fill the shops;
computers are also for sale
Refreshments will help to revive you, then –
you can follow the Heritage Trail
Arts and craft centres, the library, too,
and museum can fill up your day
An indoor sports centre offers plenty to do
for those with enough time to play

Buses and main line trains come from all over,
including a branch line from Looe
As will be found, this old market town thrives,
as it integrates everything new
Mary Portas's programme on national T.V.
was a gift to the town there's no doubt
It was, as she claims, just *a catalyst* that
would bring all of our ideas out

Mary's been slammed by an M.P. who called her
"nostalgic and foolish" (how rude!)
But he should come here and find out for himself
she's not foolish – it seems she is shrewd

RAINY DAYS

I stand by the window and watch the pouring rain
It's falling like tears upon the windowpane
I haven't seen rainbows or sunshine since you went away
Life is empty and lonely and grey

Every day's a rainy day
While you have to be away
I never laugh and seldom smile
Tears are more my style

Barometers dropped when you had to go away
The hands moved to *Dull* and there they seemed to stay
But I forecast a change in the weather when eventually
We're together as we used to be

Rain and teardrops soon will dry
Nevermore we'll say "goodbye"
The sun in my heart will start to shine
When the outlook's *Fine*

REFLEXOLOGY

The joy of Reflexology experienced with Chris
Was more than I expected – coming very near to bliss

Feet held firm in healing hands assured me from the start
That when relaxed the reflex points would link to every part

Identifying where a blocked-up energy could be
Causing problems large and small that were affecting me

Powdered skin responded to the gentle probing fingers
Like silken massage on my soles – the memory still lingers

Effects can be quite sudden or more subtle in their turn
Whatever the results for me I know that I'll return

This feeling of wellbeing that's now delighting me
Can be maintained with Chris's lovely Reflexology

ROWING ON THE FOWEY

Launching at Lostwithiel
Early in the day
Rowing on the ebbing tide
He soon gets under way

Isolated by the mist
It's peaceful on the Fowey
A dream world like the one he knew
When he was just a boy

Once the sun burns off the mist
He sees the wider view
Gently rolling countryside
An animal or two

As the river nears the sea
His work is nearly done
He'll go home later in the day
When the flood tide starts to run

Once his boat is made shipshape
He heads off into town
For a longed-for lunch of fish and chips
And a drink to wash it down

SENSES

Words are like the paint upon an artist's brush for me
To colour the portrayal of the scenes that I can see
Describing how the blazing sun makes shadows leap and play
Then changes us from hot to cold when clouds get in the way

Dewdrops in the morning shine and glisten in the sun
Looking like real diamonds, delighting everyone
Yet how can those who cannot see envisage such delight
Unless some words can capture all that's hidden from their sight

Can poems paint a rainbow that will help the blind to know
How blooms reflect its colours and create a gorgeous show
Does smelling flowers or walking through a field of new mown hay
Stimulate their senses in a very different way

Although we cannot see the wind we feel it when it blows
And when it's cold and frosty we can sense it with our nose
Our feet enjoy a tickle when we paddle in the sea
And we love the taste of toast and jam when we come home for tea

The sound of rushing waterfalls or babbling of a stream
Can tantalise a person's soul and activate a dream
Dreaming has our senses uncontrolled and running wild
Opening up the magic world we found when just a child

It's said a picture's worth a million words, which may be true
When looking at Old Masters or observing something new
To paraphrase this saying that's been here a long long time
A million words can paint a lot of pictures in the mind

SILENCE

Quiet man of the moor
Freedom to roam, time all his own
Walking tirelessly, in tune with the moor
Harsh, mystical, beautiful, always inspirational
Miles and miles to explore

In silence

Solace found in solitude, the dawn light,
Sunsets, gale-force winds,
Balmy breezes, the eerie stillness of no wind
Moonlight on Hawks Tor
Emotions find voice
Crying out in the emptiness "This is mine"

Then silence

Clouds hide the moon
Darkness absorbs him
Into a secret world
Of night creatures

And silence

SING A SONG

Sing a song in wartime
That's what they used to do
Trying to put their cares aside
And keep on smiling through

Sing a song of sadness
Young lovers had to part
They never knew if they'd survive
To marry their sweetheart

Sing a song of hopefulness
The war was nearly won
Families soon would welcome home
Their men and have some fun

Sing a song of peacetime
They all sang "Hip Hooray"
Yet rationing and shortages
Seem endlessly to stay

We now sing of prosperity
It's quite a different life
Built on foundations laid for us
In those dreadful years of strife

SNOW

Snow has fallen overnight
Everywhere is brilliant white

Like a feather duster clearing air
Of pollution and gasses lurking there

Rooftops have a quilt of snow
So have the gardens down below

Birds are circling overhead
Looking to see who's left out bread

Footprints clearly stating that
Their food's attractive to a cat

Leaden clouds now passing by
Glimpses of bright blue in the sky

Snow on the trees begins to thaw
Transformation's watched with awe.

Snow caused disruption all over town
But best of all we all slowed down.

If snow brings messages from above
They must be of beauty and come with love

Earth's nourished by the heavenly snow
And so are we, for all we know

SOMETHING BEAUTIFUL

The thought of something beautiful on a cold and rainy day
helps to lift the spirits and drive the blues away

Thinking of the children and their gorgeous baby ways
brings lovely memories floating back of those far off happy days

The garden in the springtime with blossoms bulbs and trees
are joyful recollections always guaranteed to please

To feel the warmth of sunshine when I think of sand and sea
remembering family holidays and the pleasure they gave me

There are also precious letters from loved ones far and near
by now I know the words by heart and they echo loud and clear

With memories that are beautiful I even welcome rain
it means I'll have a quiet time to recall them once again

SOMEWHERE ELSE

All of the people in their cars
Are driving to somewhere else
Passengers boarding aeroplanes
Will quickly be somewhere else

Refugees leaving homes behind
Are forced to be somewhere else
Tourists and hikers young and old
Are heading for somewhere else

People all seem so unsettled
And need to be somewhere else
Ambitious men who are aiming high
Strive to be somewhere else

Even babies and children seem restless
Do they feel they should be somewhere else
And parents persuaded by adverts
Plan their holidays somewhere else

It's not just today but all through our lives
This yearning is burning for somewhere else
Although we may seek it far and wide
Should we look deep inside to find somewhere else

SPRING FLOWERS

A hyacinth of purest white
Emerged from leaves and stood upright
Six petals opened on each bloom
Exuding perfume in the room

Daffodils in shades of yellow
Seemed to smile as I said "Hello"
Frilly petals of pink and peach
Exotic but they're within reach

The native primrose spread its seeds
And now appears like welcome weeds
Each primrose lasts for weeks on end
Visiting like a favourite friend

Magnolias and clematis shout
Their beauty as they all come out
Other shrubs are blooming too
Enhancing every point of view

Despite the wind and sudden showers
Spring brings out the lovely flowers
Stored in Mother Nature's banks
She shares her treasures for which our thanks

STORMY WEATHER: 2013-14

December started out quite mild with roses still in bloom
Then coming up to Christmas gales brought misery and gloom

Roads were being flooded, power lines by trees brought down
There were blackouts over Yuletide in countryside and town

In New Year there was worse to come, gales moved in from the sea
Bringing monster waves of forty feet, spectacular to see

Their force smashed walls and promenades, wrecked boats that sank below
Buildings ripped apart could not survive the fatal blow

Those who lived in Somerset found themselves marooned again
Drainage on the Levels could not cope with all the rain

Water was relentless drowning land and flooding home
Stock was moved to safety, fearing worse was yet to come

Seas washed away the railway line, rails dangled in the air
The Penzance/London line was closed for re-build and repair

Spring tides increased the problems and were fought by folk at Looe
But they couldn't stop the knee-deep floods, what else could people do?

The Severn's overwhelmed by rivers draining land upstream
Everywhere is threatened by the gales that are extreme

Now we hear alarming news, the Thames is flooding too
It's starting to look desperate – is this "Great Flood No.2"?

(Cont'd)

Well into February there was still torrential rain
As storm clouds gathered up the sea and threw it down again

At last the politicians saw the hardships now endured
And made huge funds available so relief could be assured

Sympathetic farmers brought great loads of food and straw
To grateful victims for the stock where suffering was raw

Valentine's Day has come and gone, no parties here that night
Few ventured out as worse storms raged – no end yet seemed in sight.

That weekend glimpses of blue sky and sunshine made us smile
Had weathermen got the forecast wrong? Was there respite for awhile?

For two nights clear skies let us see the full moon shining bright
On Monday morn rain came again – a most unwelcome sight

As sun appeared more frequently and storm clouds had passed by
Normal routines would resume once everywhere was dry

Repairs and compensation costs can always be assessed
But what about the broken hearts and those now dispossessed

STANDING BY

I've been around since you were born
But I wasn't needed then
While you were young and innocent
Untouched by the sins of men

As you grew I took more notice
Of your childish fun and pranks
They didn't cause much trouble
And for that I give my thanks

The teen years brought temptations
Discovering all life's treasure
I hoped to keep you free from harm
While enjoying work and leisure

Now you've reached maturity
I'm with you every day
To help you make decisions
And to guide you on your way

"What's that?" you say, "I don't know you"
"Oh, yes you do", say I
"Although you cannot see me
I'm your conscience, standing by"

STUART HOUSE, Liskeard

This old house has been here for 500 years
Home to MPs and Mayors of the town
Host to the King in the Civil War strife
That led to him losing his crown

In the 1980's some thought it should go
But a shocked group resisted the plan
And set about raising the money to buy
Then the big restoration began

From top to the bottom it needed repair
There were new regulations to meet
A full survey scheduled the work to be done
And we saw it would be quite a feat

Completed in stages across several years
Fixing roof and re-hanging each slate
Repairing the floors the windows & doors
And restoring the old iron gate

Grants were secured for all the main jobs
Plus members' skills volunteered free
Completing the painting and cleaning required
To achieve the results that we see

A centre for heritage and arts in the town
Through the year it is open to all
Exhibitions, the 'Old Kitchen Café', too
Where a welcome's assured when you call

THANKS

Thanks for the memories of Canada this year
Champagne, schnapps and beer
With family and friends who I'll forever hold most dear
How lovely it was
Thanks for the memories, Toronto from the plane
Niagara in the rain
The trip to Campbell River – to leave them was a shame
How lovely they were
Visiting Langley was super
Vancouver seen briefly, then we're
Off over the Hurley to Goldbridge,
Gun Lake, Bralorne and Pioneer
Thanks for the memories of mountains, lakes and seas
Highways shops and trees
Chilliwack and Cultus Lake evoke more memories
So thank you, so much
Thanks for the memories of homemade jams galore
Goodies from the store
The corn and garden veggies until I could eat no more
How lovely it was
Thanks for the memories of lemon pie and roast
Salmon from the coast,
The pancakes, maple syrup, eggs and bacon and French toast
How lovely they were
I said goodbye all too often
With tears of both joy and regret
I had so much fun while it lasted
Those golden days I wont forget
And thanks for the memories of days spent long ago
In sunshine or in snow, at school, at home, on holidays,
I'll never let them go
I'm very glad I met you
And now say a fond adieu
And thank you, so much

THEY

They came from the city. They came from the town
They had left behind work. They no longer felt down
They came into Cornwall. They came for a while
They came for vacations. They lived life in style

They came in the summer. They played in the sea
They had no restrictions. They loved to be free
They thought they would work. They wanted to stay
They found unemployment. They learnt the hard way

They listened to locals. They saw life was hard
They laboured for little. They played their last card
They boarded a vessel. They crossed the blue sea
They were like men before them. They had to be free

They made a new life. They are paid a good wage
They built a fine home. They turned a new page
They left the Old Country. They left all their kin
They have no regrets. They've the spirit to win

THOUGHTS ON CREATION

In the beginning – chaos
Universe in turmoil –
Fire, storms, floods, earthquakes, volcanoes
From which our world evolved

Elements of creation
Encrypted forever in our DNA
Passed on by each generation as
Love, rage, passion, tears

Global evolution still moulds humanity
Responding, reacting for survival
Fleeing from quaking earth and volcanic mountains
Man seeks new beginnings

Invisible enemies rage in the heavens –
A noisy battleground
Relentless oceans rise eroding shorelines
Driving man to safer ground – for the time being

Occasional respite found in sunny skies
Balmy breezes and calm seas
Appreciation of earth's fruitfulness
And a peace beyond understanding

Short-lived, man is again tossed around on the sea of life
Falling in and out of love
As he becomes a player in the evolutionary game
Driven to mate and procreate   (cont'd)

Echoing original creation, elements can be spectacular
Awesome, frightening, wonderful
A child conceived. A child born.
Pain. Joy. Fulfilment

A new life in the evolutionary process
How will the DNA of millions of years be revealed
Intelligent? Purposeful? Contributing to mankind, or
Dull, useless and a drain on society

Do DNA elements change their potency
Dividing with each generation?
Do they parallel homeopathy –
Increasing potency with every birth

- For better, or for worse!

TRURO RIVER SUNSET

As the sun started setting on a cool winter day
The sight of a sunset made us hurry away
From the centre of town where it's all spend and pay
To the banks of the Truro River

The scene was set up as if placed by a hand
With every component perfectly planned
In the foreground Scots pines formed a loose-woven band
Through which shone the Truro River

The river reflected the pale golden sky
Like a mirror – its beauty was balm to the eye
The boats were at anchor, the breeze a mere sigh
Nothing moved on the Truro River

It couldn't last long – sunsets quickly grow old
Then lights from the streets began to unfold
With a final bright flourish adding highlights of gold
As night fell on the Truro River

Pictures created before us that night
Soon faded away and were lost out of sight
Replaced very soon by the silvery light
Of the moon on the Truro River

WALKING AND TALKING

The time that we treasure for having a talk
Is when we're together and out for a walk
Sharing our differing points of view
Outdoors in the open – just me and you

We don't only chatter of everyday things
But the wonder and magic of butterfly wings
The meaning of life and the beauty around
Our thoughts soar on high or stay here on the ground

Daydreaming takes us to lands overseas
Or places much closer – wherever we please
We've planned home and garden, work and our leisure
As partners for life walking's been a real pleasure

We rest for a while in a quiet shady nook
And you tell me ideas that you've had for a book
A romantic novel based on our life
A story of lovers who are now man and wife

WEATHER – December 2012

A Sunday in December, sunshine streaming in a room
that overlooked a garden where some flowers were still in bloom

As had happened now for weeks, night brought torrential rain
followed by a glowing dawn that raised our hopes again

Raindrops sparkled in the sun upon each shrub and tree
like Christmas decorations - a joy for all to see

But it wasn't meant to last for long, clouds rolled in from the west
upsetting outdoor plans again; it's useless to protest

Rain's been flooding homes and roads and washing cliffs away
best heed the warnings given and stay indoors today

As Yuletide comes much closer record rainfalls drench the ground
making transportation difficult for everyone around

Are these the changes talked about by seers in days of yore
We hope things will get better - what have the fates in store?

WEDDING OF THE YEAR

New Duke and Duchess
Married today
Millions of people
On holiday

Pageant and splendour
All going well
Horses and carriages
Casting a spell

RAF fly-past
Old and the new
Hovering 'copter
Salute from the crew

Palace appearance
Memorable kisses
Long life and happiness
To Mr and Mrs

WEDDING TREE

Lost Gardens of Heligan revealed to me
The custom of planting a Wedding Tree

Two different saplings go into one hole
Growing together in body and soul

Trunks merge but the branches stay true to their roots
Just like a couple, who produce different shoots

Life's tree gathers strength, reaching up, growing tall
Not knowing what tragedy may befall

One of the pair dies, their wedding tree's down
But life still lives on in the roots underground

Nature regenerates in man, like the tree
In his roots he's recovering where no one can see

From the roots spring the new shoots that echo at last
The life of the old tree whose time has now passed

With space to develop and reach for the sky
Young growth matures quickly, its targets set high

Man may be quite different and find a new role
Emerging from grief with renewed heart and soul

WHISPERINGS OF ETERNITY

Curtains of the night now fall
Bidding goodnight to the sun
Again the world is settling down
As bedtime has begun

Stars and moon begin to shine
Casting their silver beams
Whisperings of eternity
Then steal into our dreams

Dreaming in the moonlight
I feel a warm embrace
The love I feel is very real
I'm in a wonderful place

Dreams are of my true love
Far across the sea
He'll be wishing on the moon
And dreaming just like me

WILD CATS OF THE MOORS

Wild Cats of the moors
Roaming the valleys climbing the tors
Wild cats seeking your prey
Hunting at night time hiding by day

Wild cats seen in the moonlight
Vague silhouettes fade out of sight
Wild cats you've made it your home
If you want to stay there take care where you roam

Wild cats be ready to flee
The papers are saying guns hunt for a fee
Wild cats cheat them of their bounty
You'll find many places to hide in the county

Wild cats be wary of man
Follow your instincts survive if you can
Wild cats stay safe on the moors
The moors have their secrets the moors will keep yours

WINTER DAY

Parking in our favourite place
A spot we know so well
Landscape blurred by misty rain
But still it casts its spell

We walked these lanes in springtime
Saw bluebells bloom and die
Paddled our feet in the river
Danced 'neath the moon in July

Gathering autumn berries
Enjoying the leaves as they fall
We picked up shiny conkers
Chanting "Love will conquer all"

Now we're picnicking in the car
On a cold December day
Playing our favourite music
We're in love – what more need I say

1	Title and Welcome	52	Love and Beauty
2	Publisher	53	Magic of a Rose Bush
3	Art Show	54	Makeover
4	Autumn Love	55	Man and his Boat
5	Bards of the Cornish Gorsedh	56	Mary Newman's Garden
6	Benediction	57	Mining Landscape
7	Beside the Pond	58	Moyclare
8	Bluebell Wood	59	Music of Love
9	Bodmin Moor	60	My Acers
10	Boundaries	61	(cont'd)
11	Carnglaze Cavern	62	My Acers – Adieu October Glory
12	Christmas Weather 2013	63	Musician
13	Cornish Heritage	64	Mysteries
14	Cornish Gardens	65	New Beginnings
15	(cont'd)	66	New Home
16	Dawn	67	November in the Garden
17	Deciduous Azaleas	68	Now I am Old
18	Deep in my Memory	69	Olympic Torch Relay
19	Dehwelans	70	On a Sunny Day
20	Elusive Words	71	On the Ocean of Life
21	Empty House	72	Only a Fragment
22	Enchanted Garden	73	Paris in Spring
	Fascination of Cornwall	74	Perfect day in Cornwall
23	WATER	75	Perfect Vision
24	ROCKS	76	Portas Pilot Scheme
25	MOORLAND	77	(cont'd)
26	February Flowers	78	Rainy Days
27	Flights of Fancy	79	Reflexology
28	Foggy Day in Cornwall	80	Rowing on the Fowey
29	Full Moon	81	Senses
30	Garden Volunteers	82	Silence
31	Gardening 2012	83	Sing a Song
32	Going Home	84	Snow
33	Grannies	85	Something Beautiful
34	Grief	86	Somewhere Else
35	Guardian Angel	87	Spring Flowers
36	Harmony in the World	88	Stormy Weather 2013/14
37	Henry Rice	89	(cont'd)
38	Hey Dad !	90	Standing By
39	Hidden Garden	91	Stuart House
40	Holding Hands	92	Thanks
41	Holiday in Canada	93	They
42	Holiday Magic	94	Thoughts on Creation
43	Hyacinths	95	(cont'd)
44	I'll Never Forget Canada	96	Truro River Sunset
45	In my Garden January 2012	97	Walking and Talking
46	I.T. Wizard	98	Weather – December 2012
47	It's Summer	99	Wedding of the Year
48	January Camellias	100	Wedding Tree
49	Knowing	101	Whisperings of Eternity
50	Liskeard O.C.S.	102	Wild Cats of the Moor
51	Living the Dream	103	Winter Day